Table Of Contents

Overcoming Procrastination: An Ultimate Guidebook to Doing The Right Thing At The Right Time.

Introduction

Dive into a life-transforming journey with "Overcoming Procrastination: An Ultimate Guidebook to Doing The Right Thing At The Right Time." Unleash your potential, break free from the chains of procrastination, and seize every opportunity that life offers!
In this revolutionary guide, discover:

- Proven strategies to conquer procrastination and boost productivity.
- The psychology behind procrastination, unravelling the mysteries of your mind.

- Practical tips to prioritize tasks effectively and create a roadmap to success.
- Empowering stories of individuals who turned their lives around by defeating procrastination.
- Actionable steps to build resilience, discipline, and a winning mindset.

Say goodbye to missed deadlines and unrealized dreams. It's time to take control! Don't just dream about a more productive, fulfilling life—make it a reality! Grab your copy now and embark on a journey to unlock your true potential. The first step to success is just a page away!

 #NoMoreProcrastination
#TakeChargeToday

Understanding Procrastination

In the labyrinth of personal development, understanding procrastination is the compass guiding us toward self-mastery. In this chapter, we embark on a psychological odyssey, unravelling the intricate threads that weave the procrastination tapestry. It's not merely about delay; it's about decoding the intricate dance between intention and action.

Delving into the psychology behind procrastination, we confront the inner workings of the human mind, where motivations, fears, and desires create a complex symphony. As we dissect the layers, readers will discover that procrastination is not a mere flaw but a nuanced response to a myriad of emotional and cognitive triggers.

From the subtle whispers of self-doubt to the siren call of instant gratification, we examine the cognitive biases that fuel procrastination. By identifying these triggers, readers gain a profound awareness, transforming procrastination from an elusive adversary to a conquerable foe.

Furthermore, we explore the profound consequences of procrastination, shedding light on the toll it takes on personal and professional growth. Through poignant stories and real-life examples, readers witness the tangible impact of procrastination on dreams deferred and opportunities lost.

This chapter is not a mere exploration; it's a call to self-discovery and empowerment. Armed with knowledge, readers will emerge equipped to intercept procrastination at its roots, fostering a proactive mindset that paves the way for a more purposeful, productive life. As the journey unfolds, the fog of uncertainty lifts, revealing the path to overcoming procrastination and unlocking the door to untold possibilities. Welcome to the gateway of transformation.

The Psychology Behind Procrastination

In the intricate landscape of human behaviour, procrastination emerges as a psychological labyrinth, and understanding its underpinnings requires a voyage into the recesses of the mind. The psychology behind procrastination is a captivating exploration of the intricate interplay between motivation, emotion, and cognitive processes.

At its core, procrastination is often rooted in the human tendency to prioritize short-term rewards over long-term goals—a manifestation of what psychologists term temporal discounting. The allure of immediate pleasure or relief becomes a gravitational force, pulling individuals away from tasks that demand delayed gratification. This tendency is accentuated by the omnipresence of distractions in the modern world, further complicating our ability to stay focused.

Psychological theories such as the 'Affective Model' shed light on the emotional aspect of procrastination. Here, the emotional distress associated with a task becomes a potent force steering individuals away from it. Fear of failure, perfectionism, or even the sheer magnitude of a task can trigger anxiety, leading to a subconscious avoidance mechanism.

Moreover, the 'Cognitive Dissonance Theory' posits that individuals experience discomfort when faced with conflicting thoughts, such as the desire to achieve a goal and the anxiety associated with the effort required. Procrastination, in this context, becomes a subconscious attempt to alleviate this discomfort by postponing the task.

The 'Expectancy-Value Theory delves into the belief that success is achievable and the value one places on the task. When individuals doubt their capabilities or perceive a task as unimportant, the motivation to initiate action dwindles, paving the way for procrastination to take root.
As we navigate the intricacies of the psychology behind procrastination, readers gain a profound understanding of their internal landscapes. Armed with

this knowledge, they are not merely bystanders to their procrastination tendencies but empowered architects of change, capable of reshaping their cognitive and emotional responses. This exploration is not just a journey into understanding procrastination; it is a transformative odyssey toward self-awareness and proactive change. Identifying Procrastination Triggers Identifying procrastination triggers is akin to deciphering a personalized code within the intricate machinery of the mind. It involves a deep introspective dive into the subtle cues and intricate mechanisms that set the procrastination wheels in motion. The journey toward overcoming procrastination begins with the mastery of recognizing these triggers, a skill that not only unveils the roots of procrastination but also arms individuals with the power to disrupt its patterns.

One significant trigger is the insidious whisper of self-doubt. When individuals question their abilities or succumb to the fear of failure, the looming task transforms from a manageable challenge into an overwhelming mountain. This psychological barrier becomes a breeding ground for procrastination, as the mind seeks refuge in delay to avoid the discomfort of facing potential inadequacy. Perfectionism, often hailed as a virtue, reveals its darker side as a potent procrastination trigger. When the pursuit of flawlessness becomes paralyzing, individuals may find themselves immobilized by the fear of not meeting impossibly high standards. The result is a postponement of action, a hesitancy born from the belief that anything less than perfection is unworthy.

Task aversion, another trigger, emerges when a task is perceived as unenjoyable, boring, or uninteresting. The mind rebels against the perceived monotony, seeking refuge in more instantly gratifying activities. The allure of short-term pleasure, whether in the form of social media, entertainment, or other distractions, becomes a powerful force diverting attention away from the task at hand.

Recognizing these triggers is a transformative act. It empowers individuals to intercept procrastination at its inception, dismantling the subconscious barriers that impede progress. Armed with this self-awareness, readers can navigate their mental landscapes with precision, dismantling procrastination triggers and replacing them with proactive, purpose-driven responses. The journey from identification to liberation is not just an intellectual exercise; it is a practical roadmap toward reclaiming control and embracing a life of meaningful action.

The Procrastination Pitfall

Embarking on the exploration of procrastination, one must confront the treacherous terrain of the procrastination pitfall—a landscape where intentions often crumble in the face of hesitation and opportunities slip through the fingers of deferred action.

The procrastination pitfall is not a mere delay in tasks; it is a perilous plunge into the abyss of missed potential and unrealized dreams. As we peer into its depths, we encounter the multifaceted consequences that echo through personal and professional realms. Missed deadlines, unfulfilled ambitions, and the erosion of self-confidence are but a few of the shadows cast by the procrastination pitfall.

This chapter serves as a stark revelation, illuminating the true cost of procrastination. It unveils the toll it takes on the architecture of success, dismantling the scaffolding of achievements one delay at a time. Through poignant narratives and real-world examples, readers witness the tangible impact of procrastination on careers left unfulfilled and aspirations relegated to the shadows.

Yet, within the pitfall lies the potential for redemption. It becomes a crucible for transformation, a space where the gravity of consequences propels individuals to confront the urgency of change. It is not a condemnation but an invitation—a call to ascend from the depths, armed with newfound clarity and purpose.

As we navigate the procrastination pitfall, readers are beckoned to face the uncomfortable truths, understanding that the cost of inaction surpasses the discomfort of tackling tasks head-on. This chapter is not just an acknowledgement of the pitfall; it is the first step towards a strategic ascent, a journey out of procrastination's grasp and into the sunlight of productivity and fulfilment. Welcome to the precipice of change.

Consequences of Procrastination

The consequences of procrastination, within the shadowy realm of the procrastination pitfall, unfold as a cautionary tale of deferred actions and missed opportunities. It's not merely a delay but a domino effect that reverberates through various facets of life, leaving a trail of unfulfilled potential in its wake.

At its core, procrastination takes a toll on the temporal landscape. Missed deadlines, once markers of promise, transform into signposts of opportunities forfeited. This temporal erosion, compounded over time, can lead to a sense of stagnation, leaving individuals standing still in a fast-paced world.

Professionally, the consequences are palpable. Unfinished projects and delayed tasks chip away at the foundation of success. Careers that could have soared find themselves tethered to mediocrity. The procrastination pitfall becomes a career impediment, hindering progress and relegating ambitious goals to the status of mere aspirations.

On a personal level, the emotional toll is profound. The constant companion of unmet deadlines, coupled with the awareness of potential unfulfilled, breeds self-doubt. The erosion of self-confidence becomes collateral damage of procrastination, as individuals grapple with the gap between their aspirations and the reality of inaction.

Moreover, procrastination can strain relationships. Unkept promises and unfulfilled commitments sow the seeds of distrust. The repercussions extend beyond the individual, affecting collaborative efforts and partnerships.

Yet, within this litany of consequences lies an opportunity for redemption. Understanding the full scope of the procrastination pitfall catalyzes change. It's a call to action, urging individuals to confront the discomfort of tasks head-on, for the cost of inaction surpasses the transient comfort of delay.

This chapter does not merely illuminate the consequences of procrastination; it serves as a rallying cry for transformation. It invites readers to acknowledge the gravity of the pitfall, embrace the discomfort of change, and rewrite the narrative of their lives. The consequences are not an endpoint but a crossroads—a juncture where proactive choices can redefine the trajectory of success and fulfilment.

Breaking the Cycle

"Breaking the Cycle" within the realm of the procrastination pitfall is a call to disrupt the repetitive patterns that bind individuals to the shackles of inaction. It's a pivotal moment in the narrative, where the awareness of consequences transforms into a catalyst for change, propelling individuals toward a future untethered by the chains of procrastination.

Breaking the cycle begins with a deep introspective journey. It involves unravelling the threads of habitual delay and understanding the root causes that perpetuate the procrastination loop. Whether fueled by fear, self-doubt, or the allure of momentary comfort, these cycles must be identified and dissected.

The power to break the cycle lies in cultivating a proactive mindset. It's about redefining one's relationship with tasks, shifting from avoidance to engagement. Embracing discomfort becomes a conscious choice, recognizing that the temporary unease of action is far preferable to the enduring regret of inaction.

Strategic planning becomes a cornerstone in breaking the cycle. Setting realistic goals, breaking them into manageable steps, and creating a roadmap for success provide a structured approach to tackling procrastination head-on. This method not only mitigates the overwhelming nature of tasks but also instils a sense of accomplishment with each small victory.

Moreover, breaking the cycle involves rewriting the narrative of failure. Understanding that setbacks are not synonymous with defeat reframes the perception of challenges. Rather than viewing failures as insurmountable roadblocks, they become stepping stones toward growth and resilience.

This chapter serves as a guide through this transformative process. It

illuminates the path to breaking free
from the procrastination cycle, urging
readers to recognize the agency they
possess in shaping their destinies. It's
not just about breaking free from the
chains; it's about forging a new,
empowered identity—one that thrives in
the face of challenges, embraces
discomfort, and charts a course toward
a future defined by proactive choices
and fulfilled aspirations.

Mindset Makeover

"Mindset Makeover" marks a pivotal
chapter in the journey of overcoming
procrastination, where the
transformation from inertia to initiative
begins at the core of one's beliefs and
attitudes. This section delves into the

intricate landscape of cultivating a proactive mindset—an indispensable tool for dismantling the procrastination stronghold.

At its essence, a mindset makeover involves a shift from a reactive stance to a proactive approach. It's not merely about completing tasks but fundamentally altering the lens through which challenges are perceived. The chapter explores the psychology behind adopting a proactive mindset, unveiling the power of positive self-talk, affirmations, and visualization in reshaping cognitive patterns.

Central to this makeover is the cultivation of self-efficacy—the belief in one's ability to succeed. Through introspective exercises and empowering narratives, readers are guided to confront and conquer self-doubt. The chapter emphasizes that procrastination often stems from a lack of confidence in one's capabilities, and a mindset makeover is an antidote to this debilitating mindset.

Furthermore, the concept of embracing discomfort is woven into the fabric of a proactive mindset. By reframing challenges as opportunities for growth and learning, individuals are encouraged to step outside their comfort zones. This shift not only diminishes the fear associated with tasks but also fosters resilience and adaptability.

The "Mindset Makeover" chapter serves as a beacon, illuminating the transformative potential that lies within the recesses of one's thoughts. It beckons readers to recognize that the journey to overcoming procrastination is not solely about mastering time management techniques but, fundamentally, about crafting a mindset that thrives on action, resilience, and an unwavering belief in one's ability to shape a purposeful and fulfilling life.

Cultivating a Proactive Mindset

"Cultivating a Proactive Mindset" emerges as the cornerstone within the transformative landscape of the "Mindset Makeover" chapter, a beacon guiding individuals from the shadows of procrastination to the brilliance of purposeful action. This subtopic unravels the intricate tapestry of thoughts, beliefs, and attitudes, empowering readers to redefine their relationship with tasks and time.

At its core, cultivating a proactive mindset involves a deliberate shift from passivity to agency. It's about acknowledging the power one holds in steering the course of their life. The chapter navigates the labyrinth of positive psychology, exploring the profound impact of thoughts on behaviour. Through engaging exercises and reflective prompts, readers embark on a journey to identify and reshape limiting beliefs, fostering a mental environment that nurtures initiative.

A key facet of this cultivation lies in the mastery of time perception. Procrastination often thrives on a distorted view of time, with tasks looming as insurmountable obstacles. By reframing time as a resource to be managed rather than an adversary to be conquered, individuals gain a newfound sense of control. This shift liberates them from the paralysis induced by the enormity of tasks, enabling a proactive approach to time utilization.

Moreover, the chapter delves into the concept of goal alignment. Cultivating a proactive mindset necessitates a clear vision of personal and professional aspirations. Readers are guided through the process of setting SMART goals—Specific, Measurable, Achievable, Relevant, and Time-bound—creating a roadmap that transforms aspirations into actionable steps.

In essence, "Cultivating a Proactive Mindset" transcends the conventional understanding of time management. It's a holistic approach that recognizes the symbiotic relationship between thoughts and actions. As readers absorb the principles of proactive thinking, they become architects of their destinies, liberated from the clutches of procrastination and poised to embrace a future shaped by intention, purpose, and unwavering belief in their ability to manifest positive change.

Overcoming Self-Doubt

"Overcoming Self-Doubt" unfolds as a pivotal exploration within the expansive territory of the "Mindset Makeover" chapter, illuminating the profound impact of self-belief on the journey from procrastination to purposeful action. This subtopic invites readers to confront the insidious shadows of uncertainty that often sabotage endeavours, providing a toolkit to dismantle the barriers erected by self-doubt.

Self-doubt, a formidable adversary in the realm of personal development, is dissected with precision. The chapter unravels the intricate dance between fear and belief, exposing self-doubt as a cognitive distortion that hinders progress. Readers are guided through introspective exercises that unveil the roots of their self-doubt, whether rooted in past experiences, societal expectations, or an innate fear of failure.

Central to overcoming self-doubt is the cultivation of self-compassion—a gentle acknowledgement of one's imperfections coupled with a commitment to growth. The narrative emphasizes that self-doubt is not an immutable trait but a malleable aspect of the human psyche. Through compassionate self-reflection, individuals learn to challenge negative self-talk and reframe their internal dialogue.

Furthermore, the chapter explores the symbiotic relationship between self-efficacy and overcoming self-doubt. By celebrating small victories and acknowledging personal achievements, individuals build a reservoir of confidence that counteracts the corrosive effects of self-doubt. Real-life success stories and affirmations become beacons of inspiration, guiding readers toward a mindset characterized by belief in their capabilities.

The subtopic is a call to embrace discomfort and uncertainty as inherent aspects of the growth process. By reframing challenges as opportunities for learning and resilience, individuals begin to perceive self-doubt not as an obstacle but as a stepping stone toward personal evolution.

In essence, "Overcoming Self-Doubt" is not just a chapter—it's a guide through the labyrinth of the mind, an invitation to liberate oneself from the shackles of doubt, and a transformative journey toward a mindset rich in confidence, resilience, and an unwavering belief in one's ability to navigate the complexities of life.

Strategies for Immediate Action
"Strategies for Immediate Action" emerges as a beacon of efficacy in the quest to overcome procrastination, providing a roadmap for individuals to break free from the inertia of delay and

embrace the power of now. This chapter is not merely a collection of techniques but a profound exploration of the art of initiating immediate and purposeful action.

At its essence, strategies for immediate action involve a recalibration of one's relationship with time. The chapter delves into the psychological intricacies of procrastination, unravelling the deceptive allure of tomorrow and the seductive comfort of delay. Readers are guided through techniques that anchor their focus on the present moment, disrupting the cycle of perpetual postponement.

The Pomodoro Technique, a cornerstone in this arsenal of strategies, is unveiled as a powerful tool to enhance productivity. By breaking tasks into manageable intervals, punctuated by brief breaks, individuals not only optimize their concentration but also dismantle the overwhelming nature of large tasks.

Prioritization becomes a key theme, as readers are encouraged to discern between urgent and important tasks. The chapter advocates for a strategic approach that ensures immediate action on tasks with significant impact, preventing the accumulation of deferred responsibilities.

Moreover, the narrative unfolds the significance of creating a conducive environment for immediate action. From decluttering physical spaces to minimizing digital distractions, the strategies extend beyond the mental realm into the physical, fostering an environment that nurtures focus and facilitates swift execution.

In essence, "Strategies for Immediate Action" is a guide to reclaiming the present moment from the clutches of procrastination. It empowers individuals to view each moment as an opportunity for progress, inviting them to seize the now and transform intentions into tangible accomplishments. This chapter isn't just about defeating procrastination; it's a manifesto for a life sculpted by decisive, immediate, and purposeful action.

Prioritization Techniques

Within the profound landscape of "Strategies for Immediate Action," the subtopic of "Prioritization Techniques" emerges as a compass, guiding individuals through the labyrinth of tasks toward purposeful and timely execution. This exploration into prioritization is not just a practical guide; it's a transformative journey toward mastering the art of discernment in the face of a multitude of responsibilities.

At the heart of prioritization lies the discernment between urgency and importance. The chapter unveils the Eisenhower Matrix as a powerful tool, urging readers to categorize tasks into four quadrants: urgent and important,

important but not urgent, urgent but not important, and neither urgent nor important. This matrix becomes a roadmap for navigating the often chaotic landscape of to-dos, offering clarity on where immediate action is required and where strategic planning can unfold.

Furthermore, the narrative delves into the concept of the "Eat That Frog" philosophy, borrowing its name from a quote attributed to Mark Twain. This philosophy advocates tackling the most challenging and impactful task first, akin to eating the proverbial frog. By confronting the most daunting task at the outset, individuals not only optimize their energy but also lay the foundation for a day characterized by accomplishment.

The chapter also explores the concept of time blocking, a technique where specific time slots are allocated to distinct tasks. This deliberate segmentation of time ensures that each task, regardless of its magnitude, receives dedicated attention, minimizing the tendency to procrastinate.

In essence, "Prioritization Techniques" is a guide to navigating the sea of responsibilities with intention and efficiency. It transcends the mere management of tasks; it's a paradigm shift toward a proactive mindset that strategically allocates time and energy to tasks that align with overarching goals. Through these prioritization techniques, readers are empowered not only to conquer immediate challenges but to sculpt a trajectory that aligns with their long-term aspirations.

The Power of the Pomodoro Technique
"The Power of the Pomodoro Technique" stands as a transformative pillar within the expansive realm of "Strategies for Immediate Action," offering a time-tested method to propel individuals past the inertia of procrastination and into the rhythm of focused productivity.

At its core, the Pomodoro Technique is a simple yet profound strategy that recognizes the human mind's propensity for optimal focus within specific time intervals. Originating from the Italian word for tomato, the technique was coined by Francesco Cirillo, who initially used a kitchen timer shaped like a tomato. The concept is elegantly straightforward: work intensely for 25 minutes (a Pomodoro), followed by a short 5-minute break. After completing four Pomodoros, take a longer break of 15-30 minutes.

This structured approach to time management serves as a powerful antidote to the overwhelming nature of tasks. The ticking clock imposes a sense of urgency, prompting individuals to immerse themselves fully in the task at hand. The frequent breaks act as mental respites, preventing burnout and maintaining a sustained level of attention throughout the day.

"The Power of the Pomodoro Technique" chapter explores the psychological underpinnings of this method, unveiling its ability to enhance focus, mitigate the impact of distractions, and foster a sense of accomplishment. The ticking timer becomes a motivational cue, transforming procrastination into a race against time, with each Pomodoro representing a step closer to completion.

Moreover, the Pomodoro Technique is adaptable to various tasks and projects. Whether tackling a complex work assignment, studying for exams, or engaging in creative endeavours, the Pomodoro Technique becomes a universal key to unlocking productivity potential.

In essence, this subtopic transcends the mechanical ticking of a timer; it's a revelation of a structured rhythm that harmonizes with the natural cadence of human attention. "The Power of the Pomodoro Technique" is not just a chapter; it's an invitation to harness time as a powerful ally, transforming moments of procrastination into bursts of focused, efficient action.

"Overcoming Procrastination in Specific Areas" delves into the nuanced challenges individuals face in distinct facets of their lives, offering tailored strategies to conquer procrastination's grip. This section acknowledges that procrastination is not a monolithic barrier but manifests differently in various arenas, necessitating a targeted approach for success.

Whether grappling with work-related tasks, personal projects, or academic responsibilities, this chapter serves as a personalized guide to navigating the unique landscapes of procrastination within each domain. It recognizes the intricate interplay between individual motivations, environmental factors, and the nature of the tasks at hand.

In the professional realm, the chapter explores strategies to overcome procrastination at work. This includes techniques for time management, setting realistic goals, and fostering a proactive work environment. By addressing the specific challenges of the workplace, individuals can enhance their efficiency and job satisfaction.

For personal projects, the narrative unravels the psychological dynamics that often impede progress. Strategies encompass breaking down projects into manageable steps, leveraging accountability mechanisms, and fostering a mindset that values personal growth.

In the academic arena, the chapter addresses the unique challenges students face. From tackling assignments to preparing for exams, it offers insights into effective study habits, goal-setting, and time-blocking techniques tailored to the academic context.

By dissecting procrastination in these specific areas, the chapter provides readers with a toolbox of targeted strategies. It's an empowering guide that recognizes the diversity of challenges individuals encounter, emphasizing that overcoming procrastination is not a one-size-fits-all endeavour. Instead, it encourages a nuanced, personalized approach to reclaiming agency, fostering productivity, and unlocking untapped potential in every facet of life.

Procrastination at Work
"Procrastination at Work" unravels the intricate dynamics that often impede professional progress, offering a tailored roadmap to empower individuals within the realm of their careers. This subtopic recognizes that the workplace is a unique arena where deadlines loom, responsibilities accumulate, and the consequences of procrastination resonate beyond personal repercussions.

At its core, procrastination at work is often fueled by a confluence of factors – from task complexity to job dissatisfaction. The chapter explores the psychological underpinnings of workplace procrastination, acknowledging the impact of factors such as fear of failure, perfectionism, and the overwhelming nature of tasks.

Strategies for overcoming procrastination at work become paramount. The narrative introduces practical techniques that professionals can integrate into their daily routines. This includes the implementation of effective time management practices, breaking down projects into smaller, more manageable tasks, and setting realistic, achievable goals.

Furthermore, the chapter underscores the importance of fostering a proactive work environment. From optimizing physical workspaces to cultivating a positive workplace culture that encourages open communication and mutual support, creating conditions conducive to productivity becomes integral to overcoming procrastination.

Accountability mechanisms are also explored – from self-imposed deadlines to collaborative efforts that promote mutual responsibility. By integrating these strategies, individuals gain the tools to navigate the intricate demands of the professional sphere, transforming procrastination into proactive, purposeful action.

"Procrastination at Work" is not merely a guide; it's a compass that navigates the intricate terrain of workplace challenges. By addressing the unique dynamics of procrastination in a professional context, this chapter empowers individuals to reclaim control over their careers, enhance job satisfaction, and unlock their full potential within the ever-evolving landscape of the workplace.

Beating Procrastination in Personal Projects

"Beating Procrastination in Personal Projects" unfolds as a vital guide within the broader exploration of overcoming procrastination in specific areas, recognizing the distinctive challenges that individuals encounter when pursuing personal endeavours. This subtopic delves into the intricacies of self-motivation, goal setting, and project management within the context of personal aspirations.

Personal projects often carry a unique set of emotional stakes and intrinsic motivations. This chapter navigates the psychological landscape where procrastination thrives, addressing the underlying factors that contribute to delays in personal pursuits. Whether driven by a lack of clarity in goals, fear of imperfection, or the sheer scope of the project, this exploration provides insight into the complexities individuals face when pursuing endeavours close to their hearts.

Strategies for beating procrastination in personal projects involve a blend of self-awareness and practical tools. The narrative encourages individuals to break down their projects into smaller, more manageable tasks, making the overarching goal less daunting and fostering a sense of progress. The incorporation of deadlines, even self-imposed ones, instils a sense of urgency, counteracting the tendency to delay action indefinitely.

Moreover, the chapter delves into the significance of setting realistic and achievable goals. By aligning personal aspirations with manageable milestones, individuals can sustain motivation and celebrate incremental victories, gradually building momentum toward project completion.

The narrative emphasizes the importance of cultivating a growth mindset, encouraging individuals to view challenges as opportunities for learning and development rather than insurmountable obstacles. Techniques such as visualization and positive self-talk become powerful tools in overcoming mental barriers and fostering a mindset conducive to sustained effort.

"Beating Procrastination in Personal Projects" is not merely a guide for task completion; it's an invitation to embark

on a transformative journey of
self-discovery and achievement. By
offering both psychological insights and
practical strategies, this chapter
empowers individuals to break free from
procrastination's grip, turning personal
aspirations into tangible
accomplishments and reclaiming agency
over the pursuit of their passions.

Conclusion

Embark on a transformative journey by
putting the insights from "Overcoming
Procrastination in Specific Areas" into
practice. Whether conquering
procrastination at work or breathing life
into personal projects, the tailored
strategies provide a roadmap to reclaim

control and unlock your fullest potential. Break down tasks, set realistic goals, and cultivate a proactive mindset. Embrace the power of the Pomodoro Technique and prioritize with precision. This isn't just a book; it's a guide to infuse intention into every facet of your life. Take charge, implement these strategies, and watch as procrastination surrenders to your newfound mastery of time and productivity. Your journey to purposeful action starts now.